Why She Cheats
&
How She Gets Away With It.

By:

Angelic Artiaga

Published by: Martin & Bloomberg, Inc.
Cover Design/Graphics: Gold Starr Entertainment, Inc.
Facebook.com/WriterAngelicArtiaga
Twitter: @AngelicArtiaga
Copyright © 2015 Angelic Artiaga
All rights reserved.
ISBN-13: 978-0692621585

DEDICATION

for The Feather In My Hat...

CONTENTS

INTRODUCTION

Cheating is a matter of opinion when it comes to the game of love. On one hand it means to deceive or trick, but on the other, if you look at from a different angle or under a new light, you can see subtle details that were not there before. Personally I feel that while any game is being played and each player is playing by the same rules, there is no cheating going on.

In this book, Why She Cheats and How She Gets Away With It, I am going to break everything down to you in such detail you may find yourself wanting to throw this book against the wall because the truths that I am going to tell just may piss you off!

Some ask, "Aside from being a woman, what makes you feel that you are an authority to speak on cheating?" To them I say, I have never coined myself as "an authority" however, life experiences is what makes me one of the best sources for this information.

I come from a long line of both men and women "cheaters" and "I'm-not-cheating cheaters". Starting with my grandfather, who was a real milk man making 5 a.m. deliveries of milk and milk – if you catch my drift – to women who had cheating husbands, to my cheating aunts, and brothers, and in-laws, and family friends, and associates, and so forth and so on. I've watched them start cheating, love cheating, hate cheating, and eventually stop cheating. Hell, I know so many cheaters, even I have been a cheater, and when I did it, I would consider myself to be the best!

I've done personal studies on people and relationships. I have always been a people watcher and have made it my business to figure out what makes them tick. I've read book and became bored with them and have finally made the decision to write a book that keeps it one hundred percent real without all of the boring shit that nobody cares about.

So here it is! Straight out and hard core! Why your woman will or is cheating on you and how she will get away clean.

Now let's play!

PUBLISHER NOTES

Relationship information guide for all men to understand the method used by women who cheat and exactly how they successfully get away with it. This book will also help him realize why she cheats on him, how to stop her, and how to fix their wounded relationship before it's too late.

FIRST QUARTER
THE ORIGINAL CHASE

In the beginning of your relationship – the first quarter - you suffered from that can't eat, can't sleep type of honeymoon love. She was your everything! She consumed all of your mental space. She had you wanting to be with her every moment of your day, had you distracted at work, while hanging out with the guys, while you slept (in your dreams); you couldn't stop talking about her – that includes talking to yourself about her.

The profound level of lust and breathtaking excitement that ruled your world was crazy! The way she smiled at you and how she complimented you, the way she bragged about you to her friends and how she did it in front of you, how she smelled and flipped her hair, how she looked at you and laughed at your jokes –funny or not- was such an ego boost for you.

In return, you made her feel special. You gave chase and made promises of nothing but the best. You used well-chosen romantic phrases, all of them spoken at just the right time. You showered her with gentle attention, made her feel like you want HER and not just her body.

You remembered your lessons learned from Woman-101; tell her all the right things during sex "You're beautiful, "I love your breasts", "I love your body", "Your skin is so soft", "I'm in love with you" OR perhaps "I'm falling in love with you" OR at least "I think I'm falling in love with you." Simple sweet nothings escaped your lips just about every time you parted them. You went out of your way to make her feel in-tuned with you and you with her. It was all part of the first quarter and the Original Chase.

It was duel a shower of affection. You washed her back and she scrubbed yours. She showered your ego, you showered hers in return. She showered your libido, you showered hers in return. So long as she was willing to give, you were willing to pay for a return. Problem is your memory suddenly developed a glitch. You forgot the very reason she ever showered your ego in the first place, thus bringing you and your woman to the position where you may be standing right now. Hence, the reason I say MAYBE is because IF she is cheating, you probably haven't got a clue and you desperately need one.

Hint: Because your invitation was such an irresistible and juicy kind of great, she took the bait and accepted your first quarter Original Chase.

Think about it. The reason YOU were so happy with her –in the beginning- was because YOU made her so happy. Because YOU made her so happy; as I have said time and again; women are designed to respond to men, therefore, she reciprocated and did the same for YOU (made you happy). Continue to treat her like a Queen and she will always honor you as King. Treat her like a servant and she will poison your soup just as most servants eventually do.

Now, some have made the delusional statement that I am insinuating that the woman is inferior to the man. To those crazies I say: Stop! It is not my intention to lower the ranking of women. That is nonsense. I am a woman and everyone knows that I stand on the highest pedestal. What I am simply stating is a relationship fact, this fact having nothing to do with inferiority or lowering a woman to a level that is beneath a man. It is all about relationship connection.

The electronic responds to electricity theory. The electronic only works when connected to electricity. A heterosexual woman only works sexually when connected to a man. It is as simple as that. Relationship and response.

During this first quarter Original Chase you should have been smart enough to realize that it is not just cliché that "whatever you did to get her, you have to keep doing to keep her."

Key word: keep - Not only do you want to keep her but you want to keep getting what you got in the beginning. Keep doing what you did in the Original Chase. Just like you, women never grow tired of feeling special. While women and men are very different, they are also very much the same. Emotions of happiness, sadness, weakness, fear, love, and hate all run through similar veins.

SECOND QUARTER
MR. & MRS. COZY

This is where the pair of you are a bit more cozy with one another. At this stage in the game, you're undoubtedly still celebrating what I would like to call the honeymoon phase of your relationship.

You let your shoulders relax and in turn she lets her hair down. You're not so conscious of your 5 o'clock shadow in need of being erased and she eases up on powdering her nose in preparation for the next time she's going to see your unshaved face. I call this the "she's-pretty-much-mine and what-does-he-care" phase of the game.

This takes place somewhere around the one year mark into the relationship, the stage when you can usually set your watch by her actions and she can set hers by yours.

In a word: Predictability – synonym: boring

Although the P.S. I love yous are still soaring through the air, they are not quite the frequent fliers that they once were. Sex is still fun and very comfortable at this point. The condoms have probably gone by the wayside and so have your bringing the after-sex-warm-wet-wash-towel to your after-sex bedside.

In a word: Incivility- synonym: ungentlemanliness

Date nights are still active and pretty exciting. They may not be as romantic as those free picnics by the lake, or exhibitionistic and daring sex on the balcony, or in the parked car on the side of the freeway as traffic speeds by, or in the bathroom of one of your friends homes during a party, or on the air plane during your first trip across the pond together. But they are still exciting enough to keep a smile on her glossed up beautiful lips. That seems to be fine with her, key word here- seems.

The reason it seems to be fine is because it was just a short time ago that the original Chase was on. She holds on to the memory of your clean shaven, handsome, romantic, catering self and that causes her to accept the change that has started to rear its new 5 o'clock shadowed head.

Notice the way she may even reminisce about times past, about how she remembers this and remembers that about this time and that time you were together here and there. She will remind you of how special those days were, how wonderful you were, how happy she was, how special you made her feel.

You will gloat in that pool filled with her champagne memories and smile, taking full credit of your ability to be "The Man". But of course, if you are average, those hints will fall on deaf ears ultimately encouraging her lips to move those words over to another set of ears, one of her "best friend's" ears. And with that comes the advice of the notorious-single-woman, which could be a problem, or a male best friend, which could mean you are shit-out-of-luck because it is highly unlikely that any man wants to admit to a woman that he is just as silly as her man.

If I were you, I would definitely not want that because type relationship advice from the single-betty or a man who is ashamed to admit that he is just as capable of lacking as you are because that is an explosion of ill advice waiting to happen.

In a word: Volatility- synonym: tension

Suddenly small disagreements start sailing in from various ports, docking here and there, and coming from nobody knows where; at least that is the claim.

But keeping in mind the original Chase, she will make up with you easily. And keeping in mind the retribution of the original Chase, you make up with her easily as well. And then there is the make-up sex, and what can I say, we all know that the make-up sex can be some of the best stress relieving ish in the world!

The best part of the vexing is when the two of you take your hot blood to the bedroom and let it boil over into back-to-back voluptuous orgasms.

Key word bedroom (the predictable and sometimes unexciting bedroom, the place where you do what you do best). Fall fast asleep!

You exhaust yourself, usually falling asleep straightaway, no more pillow talk like there was during the original Chase. She lies there beside you, listing to the rhythm of your heavy breathing, eyes darting from the ceiling to your unconscious face to the shine on your shrinking penis then back to your face, and then she thinks, and thinks, and thinks.

Disagreement swept under your rug while she reverts instinctively to what she is at her core. A woman. The mental creature that moves to the pulse of her own mind. She thinks about the present, remembers the wonderful past, and then she plans.

In a word: Equanimity- synonym: repose

Hint: Make-up sex is wonderful and the little nips at one another are tiny straws. Straws that are easily flicked off of one's shoulder, but beware; a large amount of straws soon become a bale of hay and that can be a heavy load for anyone to bear.

Which brings me to one of the main reasons why your woman will look away from you when she needs to satisfy the cravings for what she is missing, for what has been neglected. Make no mistake, this has nothing to do with what she is missing from herself or from another woman or a casual friendship, but form her man, the one that she is in a romantic relationship with. The man that she is designed to respond to.

How do you avoid these four words predictability, incivility, volatility, and equanimity? The four words that all line up pretty well with one very commonly used word: neglect.

The answer is simple but not simple. Now, before I move ahead, let me say that I know that "simple but not simple" is a big confusing oxymoron, therefore, I am going to give you some examples that should help you to better understand and nip in the bud what (if you don't take action) is sure to come; your definition of her "cheating" on you.

Something that every person can relate to is personal health, be it physical or psychological health, and here are some very simple scenarios of what I am referring to:

You go out drinking last night, you party hard, crash in the bed at dawn, and you wake up a few hours later feeling awful. Your mouth is dry because you are dehydrated. Your stomach is queasy because you are dehydrated. Your head feels tight and your eyes are burning because you are dehydrated. If you have any sense at all you will know that you need to drink some water. Not soda. Not more liquor. Water. Nothing will taste as good as water right now. You will want to shake that ill feeling and fix your physical problem. You will give your body what it craves. You will hydrate yourself the best and fastest way you know how to. You will drink water. Problem attended to and now you can rest without vomit brimming at your throat.

You have sharp pains in your stomach and head because you haven't eaten in hours, you are feeling weak and tired because you are suffering from hunger pains, this drains you of energy, puts you in a bad mood, and then sends you to the kitchen or a restaurant. You want to fix the problem so you do it. You eat, and you eat until you are satisfied. Problem attended to.

Someone is arguing with you, your boss is talking to you like you are an imbecile, you have road rage amidst blaring honking horns, the baby keeps crying, the dog won't stop barking. If you are smart you will get away. You will plug your ears and move away from that situation and over to a more verbally pleasing situation. You will listen to relaxing music, the sounds of the ocean waves, or meditate in silence. By any means necessary and without thinking, you will instinctively fix your minds problem. You will not allow your mind to snap under someone else's pressure. Problem attended to.

You are lonely, you need affection, a hug, a kiss, a compliment, or some encouragement and you will get it. Some way, somehow, from someone… you will get it. If it means settling for less you will make it happen. Rather than going completely without, a little water is better than none, a little food is better than none, a little attention is better than none when it comes to your physical or emotional survival. Problem attended to.

But when you have a woman that can have more than a little, more than just enough to survive, that can have as much as she wants, there is only one thing that will stop her from getting exactly what she desires and can easily have.

In a word: Time- synonym: moment

It only takes a brief moment for the thought of a new moment to be planted into a woman's mind. However, it takes more than a moment for her to perfect her plan for enjoying that newly created moment, and like the praying mantis, women have the ability to wait for that well planned, patiently sought after, perfect moment.

Your woman is an incubator of many things. It's no wonder why she can carry a child for so long, watch the oven as the cake rises to perfection, or sit under the hair drier while conditioner moisturizes her hair. If she can do that, what would be different about her plotting her moment, the moment that you were too busy to notice developing?

Everything she does she does with the anticipation of falling in love again. And no matter how painstaking the task, she does it with ease. There is no period too long to wait when it comes to the opportunity of experiencing new and unexplainable love, as that moment is one that will be etched in her psyche forever.

The scenarios can go on and on. Think about it for a moment and put it into perspective and you will understand better how things go wrong in your relationship and how they can be stopped on a dime.

My sound advice to you –from a woman who definitely knows what she's talking about- is to avoid the moment that pushes your woman into the arms of another man.

Disclaimer: At this point I can't really say with absolute certainty that you have pushed her completely, but I am willing to bet that you have given her a little shove, she may not have budged (at this point) any further than the thoughts that may be conjured in her mind, but be rest assured that she is probably on her way out.

If you are a man who is reading this book as a preventive measure, I suggest that you stick to the original chase if you haven't stopped it.

If you are reading this book because you are just worried but not too sure, I suggest that you go back to the original Chase if you have slacked.

In either case, I need you to remember that it worked in the beginning, and it will keep working for all time.

THIRD QUARTER
HARDWOOD VS. ASPHALT

On one side of the court we have the NBA and on the other side we have Streetball. Although both are considered to be real basketball, there are some major differences in how the rules are applied.

One is professional and has created multi-millionaires displayed on national television all over the world. The other (the Streetballer) is not. He is not rich and is breaking his knees on the streets in front of few for free. Some say that the Streetball player could never hang with the professional NBA player. Some say the Streetballer is more talented and would beat the NBA player any day of the week.

But wait, before I move forward, let me say this: I am no *real* fan of basketball be it NBA or Streetball, therefore I am showing no favoritism in my opinion as I am using facts, so please put away your guillotine and don't chop my head off for what I am about to say. After looking into it and the concept of RULES, I must say that I do believe that the Streetballer is missing out on something very valuable, something that the NBA player is not. MONEY and NATIONAL SUCCESS!

Unfortunately the Streetballer is usually so undisciplined and won't learn nor conform to the rules. That's why he is not employed, showcased, or compensated on the level of the NBA player, and in order to be NBA successful, you must know the damn rules!

Sadly, the Streetballer will not be able to stack up dollar for dollar against the NBA player and we know that's a fact. It's time to ask yourself the million dollar question. Are you playing with your woman like a Streetballing player or like an NBA champion?

Rate your game:

How do you measure up? Look at the difference in players and then slot yourself. Honestly look at your game and match it to the different style of players.

The NBA player plays in a structured environment whereas the Streetballer does not really care to mentally conform to too much structure. Which are you? Do you respect the rules of your relationship? Not the new rules that you have made up but the rules that were in place from the start of the whistle blow.

The Streetballer comes with a cool slip-in-slide maneuver but that's plagued with a slim chance of not being called for a travel on the professional hardwood. Is this you? Are you slippery and always trying to get away with something slick, getting called on it in the end, and finding yourself having to try to talk you way out of it?

The Streetballer looks great doing his fancy crossovers, dunks, and alley-oops but that won't really work against a smart, well coached defense player in the NBA. Is this you? Looking good, smelling good, quick on your feet but coming up short when your woman throws up the defense move stopping you in your tracks. By the way, another way to look at this is to recognize that this only works temporarily and only on women who don't truly know who you are. Write that down!

I mean seriously, the Streetballer's many palming violations aren't called, there are no 5 second counts, and most importantly the players are not genuine defense players, therefore, a slightly good NBA defender would stop them dead in their tracks. Are your violations constantly called and defended against? Ask yourself that very important question.

On the other side of the court we have the progressive NBA and their 24 seconds violations being called as they don't allow their players to get away with wasting time. This would be your woman. She is the NBA player who gives you 24 seconds to fuck up before she calls you out on it. Is this her?

NBA players play as a team and most have some form of college education preparing them for life, and more importantly, the responsibility that comes along with having a wealthy man's career. Is she smart, have great values, comes from a background of being well schooled by a parent or a past relationship with another Streetballer where she has learned many lessons of what to and not to do? You need to understand who you are playing with.

Now don't get me wrong, I do know that there are a few dribbling cocky Streetballers that have made it from the playgrounds to the professional hardwood. There is Smush Parker, Sebastian Telfair and then there is Rafer Alston aka SKIP TO MY LOU (the best streetballer in some humble opinions) but we all know what has happened with them and him.

His individual shows have pigeon holed him as just an average player in the NBA.

Because of the core lacking of fundamentals, many of them like Jamario Moon focus more on globetrotting entertainment and showboating. And unlike the NBA player who is really shooting and defending their game, the Streetballer and his one man show does not usually bring their teams amazing success.

Disclaimer: On the topic of you can't bring great success from the streets: That, might I say, *is* a very broad statement. It's the same concept as "you can't turn a whore into a housewife" if catch my drift. I'll be the first to tell you that I've seen it done in a few cases. Let me tell you, there are a few whores out there –without mentioning any names- who have become very successful housewives; not that I am calling you a whore (huge smile) but if the shoe fits.

Back to the game.

The NBA is not perfect either. They also have poor shooters, poor sports, selfish players, etc. I'm speaking on the masses and the strict game rules to be respected if you want to stay in that game. Again, not every NBA player is incredible which brings one particular NBA star to mind. While he has a career to be envied, Shaquille O'Neal was/is not the greatest shooter, not by a long shot (no pun intended), so I don't mean to imply that you have to be perfect at all. However, poor shooter or not, he plays by the hardwood rules and doesn't switch back and forth from asphalt to hardwood, thus making him a success. Play by the rules! Be a success! Be like Shaq!

Long explanation short; both players play by similar rules, but one organization brings riches while the other keeps the player longing for riches. The most important concept - From where I sit, the sloppy selfish player will lose whereas the patient, calculated, and well coached player who is waiting and ready to yell AND1 in your face will win. Game over!

That being said, your woman will play a professional game while focusing on the weaknesses in your game. She will blindside you, she will switch up her game, she will create her own rules, and she will win! She will stop at nothing. She will leave you standing lost and confused. Whether she screams "I Win!", from the top of Mount Everest or from the private valleys of her own mind, the blood thirst affection that the woman has for personal victory holds equal power no matter how quiet her celebration.

In case you are wondering, I chose all that basketball talk because I figured you (men) would be able to relate and have a little fun while reading this reality check, and… to say this; if you switch up the rules of your game- in the middle of your game- you will likely be fouled out and benched. And, for all of you who are not basketball heads, I say this; please understand that this concept goes for all games.

If you start a game of chess and switch to checkers, do you really think that your woman is so dumb that she doesn't notice the game change? If you start a game of Backgammon and then switch to Connect Four she will most certainly notice that switch too and then you may soon find yourself playing Family Feud, Trivial Pursuit, Battleship, and eventually Operation because she will break your heart.

Just because you *neglect* – there goes that word again – to announce that you have switched from the game of Fidelity to Infidelity does not mean that she didn't notice and also made a switch without issuing an announcement of her own.

Disclaimer: You- I am not sleeping around.

Me- Infidelity is not only defined as physically sleeping around. It comes in many forms. **Objection affairs**: When one partner neglects (there goes that word again) the relationship to focus on something else – work, a video game, an intensive involvement in anything that can be detrimental to their love life. **Sexual affair**: Exactly what it sounds like. This is for sex and not usually emotional intimacy as it is strictly about nookie, nothing more. **Emotional affair**: This is when there is no smooching, but lots of sentiment and perhaps wanting to do a bit of touching. Thanks to men like Mark Zuckerberg and Jack Dorsey, the creators of our most beloved and free social media platforms, Facebook and Twitter, you spend hours on IM with someone who is not your partner, spilling all of your desires to someone who is not your wife, turning to someone else instead of your partner in times of need. This is clearly not good for your primary relationship. **Two parallel partnerships**: This is when the outside relationship is both sexual and emotional and you form a bond that feels unbreakable. You find yourself in the position where you owe the lover who is not your primary partner almost as much as you owe your primary partner. This is a person who you have fallen in love with.

Unfortunately when you play by Streetballer rules you can find yourself in one of these infidel positions and it tends to end in a position that you don't really want to play. Pay close attention to the evaluation that you have just given yourself and this will help you to address the problem and fix it. It's just like Alcoholics Anonymous, find the problem, address the problem, identify with the problem, and fix the problem.

FOURTH QUARTER
SLICK AND SLIPPERY

I know that all men are different in subtle ways, but for the most part, heterosexual men are hardwired and put together with similar nuts and bolts. If you consider yourself to have sexual desires other than heterosexual, then I am *not* talking to you, I'm talking to your friend.

Disclaimer: Due to of all of the new and creative sexual orientation terms being used today for screwing around with some women and this person and that animal and the other thing and so forth and so on, and since I don't know where your mind is and who or what you are in love with, I felt compelled to note this disclaimer.

Moving right along.

By now you may be in any length of a relationship. If you are a swift commitment then it is probably been under a year, if you are a moderate commitment then it is probably been one to two years, if you are a slow commitment then it has probably been over two years since the honeymoon stage of your relationship. You may be engaged, married, have children, or share a pet and a Netflix account, doesn't matter. What does matter is that now is the time when players are ready to play games with slip-n-slide rules.

Once things become hum drum most men start yearning for the excitement they felt during the original chase. The lust for new and illicit sex comes alive in his pants. Don't get me wrong, I understand that just because this urge may be screaming from behind your zipper it does not mean you want to end your relationship with your woman, in fact, since you have gone past the honeymoon stage of your relationship, chances are that you DO want to be with her - otherwise you would have separated by now.

At this point your eye roams and your smile broadens when you see a new prospect be it in person, in a magazine, or like many men, on your computer i.e. Facebook, Twitter, and other social media sites; *The thought of this forces me to shake my head and laugh as I'm writing this chapter.*

Nevertheless, if your eyes are roaming you had better believe that hers are too. It's like an unseen trigger. You pull the trigger and the bullet hits her. Her actions are reactive to your action. No matter how many innocent halos you try painting over your "I'm just looking" or "It's just for fun" extracurricular activities; it's an igniter that will trigger her to do the same.

The trigger that I am talking about is the *sixth sense trigger*. Don't laugh, because it is real. The energy that you exude goes through her one way or the other, positive or negative. When she committed herself to you - she became you - in a sense, in a sixth sense. It's an unexplainable feeling that she gets both when you are in and out of tune. She can't explain her romantic passions for you in the beginning and doesn't care to explain her ill suspicions of you switching your game. At his point her actions will scream louder than her words.

If you have taken a step further and have either met another woman and pursued her with phone calls, texts messages, romantic dates, and/or eventually sex (including oral sex-Bill Clinton), please get ready to swallow a huge dose of Pepto -Bismol because your woman is right on your heels and she will soon pay you the same compliment. The difference between you and your woman is that while she *may* be able to stomach your behavior, you will surely be sick to your stomach when she follows suit.

Should you be one of those men wiping sweat from your brow because you think that you have slipped under the sixth sense radar and your woman does not know what you have done - not so fast!

Just as I warned in the Hardwood vs. Asphalt section of this book, there is a 95% chance that she does know whether you came clean about your dirt or not. If she does, poor you.

To you I say; take it like a man. If you can serve it like a man, then you should be able to eat it like a man, and I hope you have a healthy appetite because she is definitely going to plate it just like she does your dinner; cooks it and serve it up to you nice and hot.

I would like to think that men would one day consider how devastated they would feel at the thought or the knowledge of another man's sex spilling between their woman's thighs or over her tongue and then make the decision to not pour his sex on another woman. Think about how your woman would feel. Put on a pair of her stilettos and then see how far you can walk in them.

If you know it would sicken you, why wouldn't it sicken her?

Let's say that you happen to be a man who has been caught by your woman and she stayed with you, why do you think she stayed? How do you think she was able to stay? Is it because she is stupid or weak? Is it because she has low self esteem and lacks confidence? Did she just have a baby or is unemployed? Or is it simply because you are God's gift to women? Whatever your conclusion, consider this one in your equation. She is *also* tolerating you because she has been, is, or is planning to be just like you.

You are a man who loves sex and you are not the only man who loves sex. That statement should mean something to you, should ring a very loud bell.

Hint: There are men everywhere who would love to give to her *something like* what you gave to the other woman. Hot, hard, fun, sneaky, and long sex. The taboo of forbidden foreplay and sex with *your* woman is the dream of the other man. Do you know why?

At this point I am going to let you use your imagination, you're a man, I'm sure you will figure that one out.

Back to what I was saying, now notice I said *something like*. The reason I said something like is because the sex that you had with the other woman was probably unplanned far in advance. For you it was a chance, spur of the moment thing, a quickie. You probably washed her smell down the drain of her bathroom sink, or the sink of a cheap motel, and for those players with a little money, down the sink of a three plus star hotel, doesn't matter. The point is that the main concern of yours was that you don't smell like her when you get home. Seconds after your orgasm exploded from the head of your penis, explosions went off in your forgetful mind. You suddenly remembered how much you love your woman and don't want to get caught. What lies you are going to tell your woman when you get home, how you are going to play it off and act cool, you may tell her how much you missed her, you may even try to have sex with her as well. Again, and unfortunately for you and for her, she will still know. If not in that moment, soon enough; a red flag will fly, she will probably be cool and calm, not make too big of a fuss, and then you do what you do best; breathe a sigh of relief before falling fast asleep like an innocent baby.

Well guess what, while you were sleeping, she was thinking.

Now that we have covered the **Why She Cheats** portion of the book, and I'm sure I have sickened you with truth. It's time to move on to the *How She Gets Away With It.*

One last **Hint**: Stern advice from me to you... Hold on to your condoms, because you are going to need them!

HOW SHE GETS AWAY WITH IT.
SHE STAYS BECAUSE SHE STRAYS

In this section of the book I am going to say things that I hope you can handle. I will also have notes for you to keep in mind. Each of these notes will be marked **NOTE**: Therefore, you can't miss them. But first I want to issue yet another disclaimer. I am not talking about every single woman in the world. While all women may be capable of what I am saying in this book – Please don't go home and act like a maniac with your woman- let's just pretend that your lovely woman is that *one* in a million. Wink!

In the first section of this book I told you the most popular reasons that she so-called *cheats* on you. Realize that I said so-called. Let's stop and define cheats: To violate rules deliberately, as in a game. Although there are a number of definitions for the word cheat, let's just go with this one since it is most fitting for the occasion.

NOTE: She so-called cheats because as far as she is concerned, after tolerating you, she feels that enjoying the company of another man… is only right according to the new rules in place of your game.

The moment YOU made the game switch she switched games too, so in her mind she is not *cheating* on you. She is simply playing your game by your rules. Remember chess and then checkers, NBA and then Streetball, fidelity and then infidelity. The old bait and switch doesn't always work; if she sees it, just like doing the tango, she will follow in step.

To make it ok and not a bad thing she rationalizes what she's doing and in turn believes that it is perfectly fine. Her belief is one of the main reasons she gets away with it. And the best part about it is that she does it with such style and grace that nothing ever really seems out of place.

Did you know that *almost* 100% of all women who have cheated never got caught? One Hundred Percent! Well it's 89% to be exact, but still, that is a staggering number.

Women also get away with it because they behave very differently from men. While you are running amuck with your fly open she is cautiously planning, calculating the exact moment that she will cradle that special man within the warmth of her Venus.

As I told you before she always follows suit, please do *not* forget that. The difference between you and her is that she wears her suit much better. She's picky and patient, takes her time browsing through racks of men, checking their fabrics, their makers, and how good he's going to make her look and feel when he is all over her.

The fuel to her tolerance is her uncanny adaptability and the satisfaction that she gets in her right-back-at-cha-baby private dance that she shares with the other man. The man that she chooses is usually nothing like you. He likely moves differently from you, speaks better than you, and holds her tighter than you do. So when you are checking for her other man and you see one that you consider to be "not her type" then blink twice because you are not looking at what she sees in him.

Another way she differs from you is taking her sweet time in making her selection. Emotionally women make plans and have strategies, while you are more impulsive. She has measured him up next to you and found that he outsize you by a long shot; and I am not only speaking physically. In some cases it may very well be physically but there are many attributes to a man that a woman is looking for that she is not getting from you.

Another of the biggest differences is that we women are much better at keeping affairs secret. We will usually brag to ourselves- if we brag at all, but men tend to beat his chest while bragging to his friends- and that friend, is what lets the wildcat out of the bag.

I once read that women are better liars because they are more psychologically sophisticated than men are. She starts by knowing you and what you are capable of doing.

If you are an insecure man it's probably because you have cheated or because you know for a fact that you suck in so many ways that there is *no* real reason she shouldn't *want* to cheat on you- and have chased her around the block and back hassling her about her every move (Q: "Where are you?" A: "Driving on the freeway." Q: "Where exactly are you on the freeway, what exit are you near?") then, oh my goodness.

Have you stooped to what lots of men call "a female level" and played Private Investigator and either social media stalked her or broke into her email or reviewed her cell phone bill or done any other DIY P.I. work?

Are you passive aggressive, controlling, suspicious or easily upset, do you question every single thing? Well you need to understand that she is aware of that and is going to use that to her advantage.

By behaving like that, you have blown your own cover. It is more than cliché that when a person is keeping tabs on their lover, chances are they are up to no good themselves. Women are smart enough to know that your insecure behavior is probably not just because you love her so much, and that it is either because of what you have going on behind her back or it's that you have realized or imagined that if you are capable of getting down in the dark that she is undoubtedly right there shadowing you and is probably doing it too.

When you get down to her budding ability to do what she does, you need to take a close look at yourself because you are definitely the root of it all. If it were not for you fertilizing that tree, there would be no blossoms. Remember she is designed to respond to you and will meet her design.

NOTE: Remember the title of this section. She stays because she strays! It's time to learn how!

THE PHONE

The ever-so-held-phone. Communication is key, therefore, this is the most important tool used in her cheating toolbox. Without her phone it would be so much more difficult for her to complete her mission. Not impossible but difficult. She must communicate in order to achieve smooth success; therefore she is going to take every precaution when it comes to how she uses this tool.

Some think that the cell phone is the root of all evil when it comes to cheating but I'm here to tell you that it is not. While the cell phone is a much more convenient communication tool, all forms of communication devices used before the invention of the cell phone has been key. Before the cell phone there was the land line, and then letters, and then smoke signals, and then hand signals, and then there were the eye signals, and before that there was the simple chance encounter where she would seduce another on the spot in the wilderness.

NOTE: There has always been a woman willing to chance everything in exchange for emotional fulfillment. From today's woman risking her failing relationship with you, to the ancient woman risking her life where she could possibly be stoned to death. There is simply no stopping a woman scorned. So please keep in mind that the cell phone is not the only tool used when slipping out on you.

NOTE: If you are an eavesdropper (on any level) or a cell phone *bill* stalker, she knows you are, therefore, you had better lift your ears and eyes away from her conversations and the *bill* and look in other places.

So for all of you DIY spies, you had better listen to me, and I mean listen carefully! If you have used any of the DIY Spy tactics she is on to you, which means she is laughing at you while whispering catch me if you can.

NOTE: Now that you have my handbook, she had better think twice about that because things just got easier for you; so Congratulations!

During a marriage/relationship (I've been married twice and in a few relationships, I won't say which marriage or relationship because I don't want to end up sued like Terry McMillian was sued for telling the world about her "men". So I will just call him my "Professor") I learned some very important lessons. I don't thank my "Professor" for anything aside from giving me world class training in the cheating arena. So without further adduce, hats off to my Professor as he was the absolute best!

One thing that stands out in my mind is how he was always watching. I had at first mistaken his tight hold on my every move for love. I mean I could not budge without him knowing exactly who, what, when, where, and why. I was so sure it was because he was so in love and couldn't live without me; I eventually realized that couldn't be further from the truth and that the real deal was because *he* always needed to be watched. He was on the lookout for two things. If he knew my exact whereabouts he would be able to gauge his chances of getting way and was trying to catch me doing, "the same thing he was doing".

By doing this he was just brilliant. He got away with so much infidelity that it's shameful. From having several women to having several children while I sat around under his watchful eye. Well, he taught me! He was so great at looking for the very thing he was doing, he got away clean. Back then he used his pager (he is not a doctor!), our and his parents house phone (before the days of *69), excuses to run to the local store, or taking an out of town job, or attending night classes, joining a bowling league (because he was stressed and needed to unwind with something fun), and every other thing you can imagine that would give him space and freedom to conquer rubbish women roaming the streets. Needless to say, I eventually I learned. I always say I have had the very best training on how to get away with cheating and I'm sticking to that one. As I said earlier, women become their environment.

NOTE: Cheat and be cheated on, love and be loved, respect and be respected. It's the circle of relationship life.

Back to her phone.

If you have access to her phone bill and have reviewed it, and/or have access to her phone bill but REFUSE her access to yours no matter what your bullshit story is (and trust me I have heard them all), or have purchased a spyware and have placed it on her phone, or have asked her to leave her phone unlocked so that you can check it at your whim, or have asked her to unlock it for you, or monitored her phone calls in anyway, then this is for you buddy. In a word: **Joke**

NOTE: When it comes to this joke you are not the one laughing, she is.

Let me remind you of another important fact. Criminals know the law just as well as -if not better than - the police. They know exactly what they can get away with and how much time they will serve if they ever get caught. I am here to let you know that if you fit any of the above descriptions, you may now consider your woman 'criminal minded' and understand that she knows your laws, so beware.

NOTE: Because she has not asked you for the same access (to your phone) *again* does not mean it's because she is okay with you refusing her. It simply means that you have just fuelled her tank of two-can-play-that-game and winner-takes-all. She undoubtedly said okay, or your right, or fine, or I understand. Any of these dismissive comments from her are dangerous. Trust me!

Sherlock, here are some of the things that your woman has done to get around you in order to enable communication with her other man/men *even* while you are watching.

Unlike so many married men or cheating boyfriends who join sites like AshleyMadisson – which by the way is not only loaded with female bots as profiles, but has recently been compromised by hackers exposing the many male members- women plan so much more carefully. She does it discreetly and keeps it to herself.

Here's her M.O., method of operation, for those of you who are not familiar with that acronym:

She has a secret prepaid phone that she hides in plain sight. She may even check the phone when you are in close proximity because she knows that the best way to keep anything out of one's sight is to leave it in plain view. We all know to be casual so that the spectators won't notice a thing; Brain Games 101. Besides that, you are so busy doing what you do with your phone, why would you notice her doing the same thing. The only way you will notice her is if you lift your eyes away from your phone and pay attention to what she is doing. But that would mean slowing down your pace of risky business.

She has identical phones with identical phone cases. Her white iPhone wearing the pink sparkly case has a twin. Because you can't help but to nose through her cell phone bill only to find phone numbers belonging to her parents, best friend, her job, her gay boyfriend, billing companies, or the pastor, you have no real concerns about who she is talking to on the phone. Therefore, if you happen to walk into the bedroom and see her talking on her pretty in pink iPhone you won't give it any thought. Your entrance is her cue to stop talking about sex and casually give her man the signal that

20

Hitler is now in her midst, "Okay daddy, I'll talk to you later, love you too." Or "Okay, I'll see everyone on Sunday."Or "Yes, the check is in the mail, thanks." She pushes end and then flashes you her 100 watt smile before running over to you and giving you a nice kiss. Mission accomplished. *She was on the phone with someone who you are comfortable with her talking to* and she is comfortable knowing that you are off her trail. Clone phone slipped into her hiding place (one of my favorites is inside a decorative bedding pillow) and off to the kitchen she goes and distracts you with a nice meal.

She has rigged her phone with many apps. Whether she is a tech junkie or not, she is technical enough to *download, install, and then uninstall* an app onto her. With today's technology it is so easy to keep the snoopers from smelling hot conversations and text messages she's really cooking up. Apps are some of the best things ever known to man and your cheating woman. They have just made things that much easier and she loves them. Many times I have found women who have adopted the Marilyn Monroe mentality. Naive acting but really as sharp as a razors edge. She wants you to believe that she is clueless and incapable of using such silly technical trinkets all the while she is a master at them. And why would she do something like that? It's simple. It is one of the many tools needed to satisfy her neglected emotional needs.

Let's talk more about apps and how important they are. Undoubtedly she has gone shopping in the mobile app market, where several developers have built programs for women and men in situations where they need to keep things top secret. If she is ready to do a little two-timing she will have gone shopping and is fully equipped with all of the communication tools she needs.

In this section, I am going to expose some of the most popular and most effective apps she is probably using. Living in this ever changing tech world, you must beware that there is a new app being born every day and so she could grab those new ones as well. The important thing is that you are aware that there is a great chance that she has some new app or apps on her side.

First, there is the standard and pretty popular Blacklist app. With the Blacklist app she is able to keep all of her secret contacts secret. By simply programming her other man's/men's phone numbers into the Blacklist she can control when he/they will and will not be able to ring her phone. When she is home, Blacklist activated. When she is away, Blacklist deactivated. Unlike you, flinching and sweating when she asks to use your cell phone because you are afraid she will find out *what she already knows*, she can let you use her phone and walk away without a second thought. Oh, and if you are looking for a particular icon on her unlocked phone that will indicated that her phone has been Blacklisted, think again.

Careful planning 101:

Alongside Blacklisting her phone there are a number of cheating apps available and being used today by clever cheaters. Here are some apps that lots of women are using, and yes that goes for your woman too - maybe-double-wink.

Listed from most clever to most common:

My top pick for most clever is the *Vaulty Stocks* app for only $9.99. At first, second, and third glance it appears to be any other stock app. It has all the graphs and numbers that any other Wall Street stock market app has going on. This is proof that you cannot always believe your lying-eyes because this app is all smoke and mirrors. An app like this is perfect for her especially since all smart phones today come stocked with a stock market app and if your woman is not the type that pays any attention to the stock market on her phone, well, why would you pay any attention to the stock market app on her phone. This is the last place that you would look while doing your detective work. It's a perfect hiding place for all of her lover's racy photos and sexy videos that she may or may not be co-starring. It is safe for her to keep in the palm of her hands for those moments when she wants to revisit them all the while keeping them private from your prying eyes.

Second, there is one app that I really got a laugh out of. The *Tiger Text* app (and others like this such as Wickr-Top Secret Messenger) ironically named after one of the most expensive cheaters yet; Tiger Woods. If only he had this one when he was cheating on his golf-club-swinging-wife, Elin. Unlike Tiger Woods, your woman will not chance getting caught or being told on by her –potentially- double crossing lover. After all, why should she trust him, I mean, he is cheating with her. With this app (Wickr-Top Secret Messenger) your woman really covers her paw tracks. Instead of relying upon him to delete evidence from his phone she does it for him. I personally think I want to nickname this one Agent Maxwell Smart because the text messages that she sends to him (including all sexy pictures and videos) will -upon *her* command-self destruct right out of *his* phone. Contrary to most men's belief, women do use men for sex and do have control of their falling-in-love emotions, therefore, when she is done with him, that's just what she wants it to be, done and over. This way when she is finished with him and he has fallen for her she will be protected. If he comes running to you in an attempt to tell on her – because they do - he will not have any proof because just like magic; 'Proof be gone!'

Then there is the *Hidden Eye* app that I absolutely love. With this app your woman can really shine the spotlight of insecurity in your face. You find yourself alone, within a few feet of her phone, it rings or not, but it is calling for your inquisitive fingers to make an attempt at unlocking her phone so that you can check out what's really going on. But fellas don't even go there because you will find yourself on candid camera. With this app the moment you try to unlock her phone and fail, the phone will quietly take your picture without giving you a chance to smile for your burglary mug shot. There is only one thing more unflattering than an off guard snap shot and that is being caught in the act of a crime-of-insecurity and having that picture of your desperate-face being shoved into your desperate-face later. Not only does this app take your picture but it has a setting on it with a very loud and piercing siren that goes off! This works better than pepper spray.

I am not and have not been a Blackberry girl for a really long time but I wouldn't feel right leaving out my Blackberry girls. This is not only about our Smart Phone girls; this book includes our Blackberry girls too. She has the Black Book app that is designed specifically for her Blackberry. With this app she keeps all of her pics, texts, and contacts in a hidden location separate from all of her pics, texts, and contacts. The beauty of this app is that even the icon for this app is hidden and the only way to make it appear is if a secret pass code is entered. It doesn't stop there. This app generously comes with a cherry on top. Should a text come through while the app is unlocked, she can program the app to have a pop out box that reads something clever like "System Memory Low" versus the name of her sexy beau.

Talking made perfect with the *Line 2* app. This app gives her a second phone number that rings to her phone. Unlike the traceable Google Voice number attached to her phone bill, Line 2 is not. It can be free or for only $9.99 she can call him without letting him know she is using an app as well. This is super easy to install and uninstall at any moment. Phone calls, sms text, photos all in one place and uninstalled when you are nearby.

For the fifth and most valuable phone covering method, the one that I cannot divulge completely is, in a word- amazing! Yes, this book is here to help you, but after all, I am a woman and do like living. I know that if I were to completely give this one away, I would be hunted and killed by some of my fellow women. Therefore, I will not give up the *name* of this particular service, but, since it is my mission to let you know how she gets away with it, I don't want to leave you completely hanging so I am going to give you a great description of what it does. If you want to look for it, be my guest. There is a service that- for a nominal fee- will unlock all of *your* phone calls and text messages and then send them directly to your woman. By the way, (It works with all android and iPhones). Now, I know that a lot of you are screaming, "Bullshit!" or "That's illegal!" well you can shout all you want, the fact still remains. You need to forget that you know *everything* and understand that it is real. First of all, your information being snatched without your permission is only illegal when being presented to and being used against you in the court of law. Not in the court of "your-woman's-opinion-of-you". I learned about this service from a woman friend of mine who used it to catch her cheating husband. All she needed was a phone number and type of phone that he had. Bingo! He was caught with no defense. Now, I can definitely see how you would find that hard to phantom especially since you are the *smartest* man on this side of the world, but it is definitely a real service.

At this point, I need you to think past your own nose. Just as any real investigation firm can tap your phone without ever touching it, any PI company can make this service available to you or your woman and any other person who would like to get their hands on it. Not only that, but for a few more bucks they will protect your woman's phone from being tapped by anyone other than a government agency equipped with a subpoena. All that to say, while you were busy sexting typos to other women, your woman was busy confirming her suspicions and protecting her own phone against you. She was making sure that you would not be able to read any of her well written sext messages to her man/men.

So now we know that what you see may not be what you get. Prepaid phone, clone phone, and trick-his-ass apps are in full swing just like Tiger's wife's golf club.

Trying to catch a woman communicating via cell phone is a lost cause. Remember the moment you let her know that you were all over her phone, she closed that door. The moment you denied her access to your phone bill, you unlocked the door to her private phone booth and planning activities.

Think about it, not only did you unlock that door when you denied her but I advise you to admit to yourself the real reason you had to deny her. Because something was going on behind her back, you switched games behind her back, and you didn't want to get caught.

Unlike you, she watched and understands you. If your woman asked to see your phone bill or call log today, your answer will more than likely be no or why because she will have caught you off guard.

Please know that the true reason she is asking is not because she wants see it, rather it is mostly to put the exclamation mark on her beliefs about you. Asking you is really a rhetorical request because she already knows exactly what's going on and that you will deny her that request.

Again, if you have ever been asked that question and your answer was no or why, just know that you have helped her to rationalize.

If you can do it she *will* do it better.

MANIPULATION

And when the woman saw that the tree was good for food, and that it was pleasant to the eyes, and a tree to be desired to make one wise, she took of the fruit thereof, and did eat, and gave also unto her husband with her; and he did eat.
~ Genesis, Chapter 3, Verse 6, King James Version of the Bible

From the beginning of time, women have been the wiser when it came to manipulating her much stronger counterpart. Remember how Eve fed Adam the fruit, and how Sarah took control of Abraham, the way Helen of Troy and her beautiful face launched a thousand ships in the Trojan War, and Catherine the Great having sexual affairs with her military chiefs in exchange for them to kill on her behalf, and of course there was the ultimate seductress Cleopatra and the power she possessed when she casted her spell on Mark Anthony with the slightest graze of her gentle touch.

If you ever suspect or accuse her you must keep in mind that manipulation is the greatest way to distract.

NOTE: Women have used manipulation as a form of survival since ancient times. She has become master and she did it under the tutelage of her man, the original MANipulator.

Men started and still manipulate with words filled with empty emotion as he is well aware that the woman is a mental creature. What he did not realize is that his tactic for manipulating his woman with words and maybe finances would backfire. By manipulating her he was teaching her how to manipulate him. Women quickly learned that words meant little to men and that —for the man- actions speak louder than words, therefore, she manipulates by offering herself up to him.

Just as you can manipulate your woman's thoughts and get her to do whatever you want just by using a few emotionally melting and romantic words like "I love you" or "You are my world". By the same token your woman can manipulate you and get you to do pretty much anything that she wants you to just by using certain actions. Here I am going to talk about a few of her most used tools of manipulation.

Touching:

Touching you is one of the most manipulative things that your woman can do. Even an amateur manipulator can be successful with this one because it is so simple. If she happens to think that you are onto her, she will turn to her number one method of manipulation to shut you up. She offers up her lady garden, the one nestled between her warm legs, the thing that you love most, the thing that is as soft as a kitten; her kryptonite to your superman. Her sex.

The power of touch should never be underestimated. All she has to do is touch you in a certain way, for a certain length of time, and then she's got you. Instantly your mind goes from suspicion to orgasm. The thought of having an orgasm is like dying and spending a few seconds in Heaven. All she has to do is open her gates to paradise and you forget all about your earthly concerns.

Unlike you needing to throw in many words with that touch, she can keep her lips sealed and you will get her intended message loud and clear. But let's say that she did use words, she only needs to use a few simple terms, and all they would have to be is something like this: "If I were sleeping with another man, would I really be touching you?" Your ego is so huge -you can't help it- it's hilarious how fast her smallest feminine touch and a few ego stroking and empty words can clip its wings.

Praising:

Praising and comparing you to all men is another trick up her sleeve. She can easily reassure your bruised ego that's dying to be revived with the almighty praises you love hearing her sing. "Why would I want another man when I have a man like you?" "He's nothing in comparison to you." Or the one that I really love is, "Are you crazy?" You have to remember that one. The "Are you crazy?" question that you have asked her so many times in the past.

Nagging:

Nagging you is another great way to throw you off. When the Nag-Hag rears her ugly head and starts bugging you about your every move you should really stop and think about that one. She has once again strategically given you a heaping spoonful of your own medicine. Unlike your nagging because you are insecure for some personal reason, she is nagging mostly because she wants you to think that she really cares about what you are doing when she really doesn't (not once she is at the point when she is also creeping). Again, the real reason she is nagging is just a matter of procedure.

Next comes the disappearance of the Nag-Hag. This is an even bigger red flag that she has something else going on. Here is the tactic. She will lose trust in you- and you know why- then she makes her decision-and I've already told you what that is.

Here is her plan:
Start nagging him about where he is and what he's doing.

Keep nagging him about where he is and what he's doing.

Cool down and make him think you are over nagging him.

Be extra nice and make him think that you have forgotten about why you were nagging him in the first place.

Let him think that he has gotten away with whatever he has done.

With a poker face, start seeing another man.

When he starts nagging her in return, grab the side of the table and then turn it hard and fast.

Once the table is turned, make him feel like the silly, crazy, delusional, imaginative, winey woman that he once claimed you to be.

Mission complete, freedom granted.

Avoiding you is another easy way that a woman gets away with seeing another man. The entire plot falls in a domino effect.

Now that she has stopped nagging you, you are ready to run and play harder. You are usually not realizing that she is giving you plenty of rope so that she can choke you with it later. You think to yourself, "Now that my woman is cool and not nagging and tripping over me so much, I can creep."

You should think again.

Her reason for not tripping is actually the polar opposite of what you think. On the contrary, this is her time to do what she wants to do without interruption. Doing this with you is the same concept as sitting a child in front of a television; the cartoons will keep him distracted; now I can get some real things accomplished.

Going to the spa:
While you are out of the way wasting time with some chick on the side she is getting some well deserved physical therapy. Women call this going to the Spa.

Think about it. Your woman tells you that she is going to some spa with her girlfriends or having some me-time at the spa with the little old lady who gives the very best massage when actually the only thing at the spa is her car left in the parking lot just in case you do a drive by to check on her.

Tactic 101:

Rambling. My back is hurting a lot lately I think I should start getting massaged. You know I read that getting massages are great for the circulatory system. I also read that massage makes the muscles pretty and soft. I really think I should start going to the spa. I think I am going to talk to (her best friend's name or her mother's name here) and ask her if she wants to go. I think it will be really good for me. I will be more relaxed and I also heard it gets rid of headaches. Maybe then I will not be so tense and will feel better about things that I have going on. What do you think? What do you think? What do you think?

After listening to all of that babbling on and on about something that is so uninteresting to you, you will encourage her to do just that. To go to the SPA! Mission accomplished.

This goes back to careful planning. She has just set the stage for the perfect (weekly) affair and she will get away with it.

The buildup

The constant chatter about it

The alibi

Remember that when it comes to an alibi women use other women and they do it for perfect reasons.

Women usually side with one another because they have experienced what your woman is complaining about.

They are paying their men back (vicariously through her paying you back)

And because (unlike your friends who will not mind sleeping with her) her alibi will be carefully selected; a woman who does not want to sleep with you.

So be it her female boss, best friend, her mother, and in some instances even her grandmother; her alibi will be air tight.

There you have it. Both men and women are very manipulative. But when it comes to being a master manipulator, women wear the platinum and diamond crown.

The subtle and natural style of a calculating woman is one to be reckoned with. I honestly believe that because women are the physically weaker of the sexes, she has had to learn how to use physical manipulation in order to maintain herself in this man's world.

And that brings me back to the world's most powerful obsession and manipulation tool that God has created: *The vagina.*

PUSSYWHIPPED

WARNING!!! The text in this section of the book is not easy to swallow and could be downright offensive to some of you guys. Not only am I a woman who knows how women think and act, I am also a writer. A real writer. A best selling erotic writer. Therefore, I will paint pictures that are not for the faint at heart. See me as your sister or any woman who is having a sit down with you about real shit that could be going on in your relationship.

We are adults here and we are talking about adult matters, and so, hold on tight and keep in mind that the words that you are about to read from here on are written with tough love for you.

The ancient woman watched as her man lost himself under the hypnosis of his harem of concubines and their vaginas. This practice of having many women has been adopted in some form throughout the ages. From Ancient Greece, Ancient Rome, in the Bible, in Judaism, Ancient China, in Thailand, in Islam, to the United States during slavery, a man having a harem of women swarming him has been a practice that all women have taken notice of, participated in, and suffered through.

I once wrote an article for Christmas suggesting that all women should give their men/husbands a sexy girlfriend or two for Christmas. Right away the male readers cheered because they imagined that I was telling their Mrs. to go out and get them a new piece of ass. On the flipside, not all, but most of my female readers understood loud and clear what I was suggesting. Keep him at home, give him what he wants, stop him from cheating, and become the concubine. That suggestion did not fall on deaf ears. Right away lights went off in the heads of so many women looking for answers to their failing relationship woes. By writing that article I was simply reminding women of what the basic desires of men have been for eons.

Soon after the article was published I started receiving reports from women of how bringing home the "new chick" to their men worked like a charm. How she took control of her relationship by simply putting on a blonde, or blue, or red, or hot pink, or jet black wig, and how pulling off the posture of the wedding-ring-wearing-prude had ignited fires in their bedrooms.

I'm sure that by now you may be asking that million dollar question, 'What does that have to do with her getting away with cheating on me?' My million dollar answer is, "It has everything to do with cheating on you."

Read carefully:

I've answered many men who have written in to my blog asking me how they can get their women to be wild or a bit wilder in bed. I say the following to you, just as I've said to them:

Every healthy woman fantasizes about being a stripper or a porn star for her man. If you have one that says she doesn't, I am here to let you know that she is lying, and you can tell her that I said it.

The women that you have chosen has undoubtedly passed herself off as a prissy little lady who believes that you are judgmental and disapproving of a wild woman, and she is afraid of falling flat on her face in front of you should she decide to do that sexy little dance that you've fantasized about or even paid strippers to do. She's afraid of being off key if she attempts to scream 'Fuck Me Harder!' or 'Faster! Faster!' in the same octave that you've heard the porn stars do while you were watching when she wasn't looking. Bottom line, it's because since you won't allow her to feel comfortable with being the stripper/porn star that lives inside her, your woman will not come out in front of you.

Your other question: "Why not?"

Here's the answer. According to many women whom I have spoken with about this, it's because of their men being childish about it. Now I do understand that men lean harder on comedy than women (example commercials during men's television programming which are filled with jokes and punchlines vs. women's television programming which is more serious and thought provoking) however… do you remember that one time when she let loose and how you made embarrassing comments or questioned her about it the next day? How you did it with laughter in your voice? How you asked her what had gotten into her? How you went about it like a fifteen year old boy? How you went about it the wrong way, when all you wanted her to say was that she had lost her damn mind because you were soooo damn AMAZING! Remember how you went fishing for compliments?

Guess what, that's the exact opposite of what you should have done. Making childish comments and asking silly questions is a turn off to most women. You should have lead with a more mature statement like, "You felt good to me last night." Or something along those lines. That way she will be happy to follow suit with a compliment to you.

I know that may sound really harsh but I'm not here to baby you or be politically correct. I am here to help fix the problem.

With that being established I suggest you listen to me because at this point I am probably close to your only hope.

First, admit to yourself that you didn't get the reaction you had hoped for and then consider the following reason:

In a nutshell, according to group discussions with several women, your teenaged-boy egotistical-reminiscing sounds a lot like an undeserving youngster who landed his first piece. Instead of reminding her that last night -as a whole- was amazing, you poked at and prodded her because you selfishly needed her to admire you, and to remind you of just how *amazing* you truly felt about *yourself* when she screamed and moaned *your* name. In a word: ***Unattractive.***

If she is outspoken and is taking your relationship seriously, she will tell you that you are silly and will probably not answer your questions. If she is shy and is taking your relationship seriously, she will probably answer you with a simple smile. If she is ready to move on to another man she will practice manipulation and will probably stroke your ego and tell you what you want to hear while whispering to herself 'don't hold your breath waiting to get that type of performance out of me again' or 'it's time for me to find a *Jonathan*?'

Because she actually loved the rough and wild sex she had with you, she is going to want it over and over again, and she will get it - minus the aftertaste of 'Please remind me of how great I was last night' or 'Wow it was strange hearing you and seeing you act that way' embarrassing moment.

Seriously think about it for a moment and put yourself in her place.

What if she said to you, 'Wow, you were moaning like you were dying last night... giggle giggle giggle' or 'What was up with those faces you were making when you were coming?' or 'This was the best you ever had right.' How would you respond to that?

Drumming my fingers...

Exactly.

You have not only introduced to her how amazing it feels to be a freak in the bed (this goes for women with less experience) but you have justified her reasons for NOT wanting to do it again with *you*. To save herself any further silly conversation with you, she does what any real pro or wannabe-pro would do. She hooks up with another pro.

Practice makes perfect.

Women love feeling sexy, being sexy, acting sexy. How can she be sexy without the help of a man? Watching movies and reading books is not enough. It takes hands on practice, and you know what they say; Practice makes perfect!

You wouldn't go to an audition without rehearsing your lines, you wouldn't run a marathon without proper conditioning, and you wouldn't go to war without fully loaded weapons and armor. Well neither would your woman. Because she is unsure of herself after getting the reaction from you that she got, she wants to be reassured so she goes for the reassurance before showing off her skills again.

While you are preoccupied with your phone and whatever else, she slips out the door and selects a man who she wants to practice being sexy with. She meets a stud she can do all of the salacious things that you think are strange for her to do. She picks a man who she doesn't have any feelings for, one she uses for experimental purposes only. She grabs a man who has something to lose; one who is probably married or in a committed relationship, a man who lives out of town, a man who probably doesn't know her real name. She commits this act with a man who is a willing teacher, and I don't mean just any teacher he is a professor holding a PhD.

From him she learns the proper techniques for incredible oral sex, anal sex, and every sexy position in between. Under his direction, she perfects how to make a man feel good. She role plays with him and its ok because he's new and doesn't really know her to judge her in the first place. This allows her to be whoever she wants to be. He shows her lots of new tricks and treats. He's there for her to perfect her craft. He can handle her and himself, is going to be on his best behavior, and will act like a *mature man* who deserves and expected what she has just given him. He is going to do a lot of what you did in the original chase.

I'm sure you are yelling, "Angie! I did not need to read all of that! What does that have to do with anything?" Well, I remind you, this is not a statistical or clinical book. I am telling you what she is doing and then following up with how she gets away with what she has done, is doing, or is planning to do. These situations are painted for you so that you can get a serious grip on reality and understand that this is real.

She comes home with her cool exterior and pretty smile on her face, playing up to you, ready to do all of the sexy things that she has done with him. She surprises you with a treat. Sex. She closes her eyes and remembers him. She opens her eyes, looks at you, but still she remembers him. She gives you all of the sexual pleasures that you ever dreamed of and more. Manipulative distraction. She does it with the confidence that he has built up in her. Now she is ready to answer your silly questions if you are crazy enough to ask them the next day. She gets away with it with the manipulation tool of touch. You want to believe it is all you (despite getting a different answer from the first time you asked her) and you turn your head and stay self centered without acknowledging the new tricks that she has brought to your and her bed. You need to recognize that the reason she simply answered your question of what got into her or your crazy comments. At this point she doesn't care about your words because her actions are much louder when she is with her *Jonathan*. Pay attention!

My advice to you: Don't ask her too many questions if you do notice the change. First of all, she will do just as you would do. She will deny, deny, deny. I suggest that you remember your fault, and let it go. Once you notice the change after you asked your usual questions, take note and don't ask any silly questions probing for compliments next time because it will send her back into the arms of her secret. If you take my advice, her romp with *Jonathan* will soon end and never happen again. You will forever be her sexy Jonathan and she will forever be your new sexy Jane.

NOTE: I know this is a tough pill to swallow because it sounds like I'm telling you to just sit back and let her get away with it. But what other choice do you have. Women have done it for years. We sit back and play our cards right and keep the relationship. Otherwise you will lose her forever or over and over again.

This type of woman calls her actions 'I did it for us' actions. She feels neglected by you but is not willing or ready to leave you completely. Remember *she stays because she strays*. She doesn't see anything wrong with parting her lips and spreading her legs for another man in the name of fixing things at home and helping her to tolerate you. This is her way of keeping her sanity. She gets to ride her sex drive out with a mature and masculine man with the hopes of gaining the confidence for teaching you a thing or two about how she wants to be treated. She does it because she is married to you, has children with you, or because she 'loves' you. Remember:

Rationalization

The drawback is that in the end she makes you do what you had her doing; questioning yourself. She makes you wonder what you were thinking when you slipped out with that other girl when you had it all at home. She has gotten away with manipulating you. Now this manipulation I like to call: Showing you the mirror. She had to show you better than she could tell you. Her actions spoke louder than her words ever could. Remember, actions speak to men. Words speak to women. Both speak to both, but one speaks more to the other. So she doesn't use very many words, she uses what works. Actions.

Bottom line she blindsided and manipulated you with sex.

She *pussywhipped* you and she did it with her *same* pussy, the only difference is that her *same* pussy has been newly trained by her other man's whip. She blinded you with sex, manipulated you with lust, showed you what she has perfected with him, and yet you are so egotistical that you think it's all about you, or you believed her when she told you that she learned how to do all those things by reading it in a damn book, and you believed her without even thinking about taking a second look at your perfect-self. In the words of Jerome Benton when he costarred in the movie Under The Cherry Moon~ *"Tisk tisk what a pity...Sometimes life can be so shitty."*

True story.

I once had a hair stylist that had been styling my hair for a few years. She had cut my hair into various styles and I loved all of them. And with that love came trust, therefore, I was never worried about how she was going to make me look.

One day I went in for my regular appointment and she asked me a simple question. "How would you like me to do your hair this time?" Well my answer was equally as simple. "Do it the same as last time." Now remember I told you that I had gone to her for years and had had various haircuts and loved them all. I mean I had some cuts that were as short as only an inch long to where my hair was on that day, which was about twelve inches long.

Because it had been quite some time since I had worn my hair in a very short cut, I assumed that when I answered her question she would realize that when I said "last" time, I meant the "last" time which was only a couple of weeks ago and not a cut from years ago.

Well, she didn't.

With my back to the mirror, she picked up the scissors and commenced to cutting my hair. No alarms went off when she grabbed the scissors because it was not unusual for her to trim my ends so that my hair would stay beautiful and healthy. Well, to my surprise, when she turned the chair around and I faced the mirror, I had my *old* one-inch hair cut! I almost died. I couldn't believe it! Needless to say, what was done was done. I paid her and left the salon in tears.

Later that evening I was with the *gentleman* that issued me those -may be harsh- words. I told him what happened and how unhappy I was about my hair. He then looked at me and said the following:

"Whatever happened to your hair is your fault; it is your responsibility to pay attention to what is going on around you and to your hair, if you want to blame anyone for what happened, you need to blame yourself. If you had checked the mirror you would have seen her scissors in action."

I didn't like hearing that, and wanted to slap him. But in a weird sort of way, he was right and those words taught me a hard life lesson that I had to master. Watch your back and own responsibility!

As harsh as those words may be, they are words that you need to hold close to your heart too. If you are thinking that I am going hard on you, imagine what women think when I talk to them about their cheating men. I preach the same sermon to them but in the reverse.

THE PHONE, MANIPULATION, PUSSYWHIPPING

These are the three main ingredients in her recipe for success when it comes to getting away with cheating on you: A dash of revenge, a pinch of studying, a heaping spoonful of planning that boils down to a thick stew of Rationalization.

Once you come to the conclusion that she is a Queen Manipulator who understands her man's psychology because she has taken the time to study him and effectively code exactly how he will react to certain situations, you will be on your way to no longer being played with YOUR OWN NEW SET OF RULES.

Remember that horrible word Rationalize? Well please understand that when any *person* is able to rationalize things that person is able to do things without any guilt or remorse.

"I walked up to him and shot him for the hell of it." Verdict: Guilty

"I shot him because he was shooting at me." Verdict: Self Defense

The first statement is foul no matter which angle you look at it. The second can be rationalized.

The first statement can reward you with a shiny pair of hand cuffs. The second can reward you with a nice handshake. The average person, no matter how mean, will usually have some flash back of the first scenario and will feel some sort of remorse. On the contrary the second scenario may experience a flashback with a smile because that person feels that their reaction was the right.

Women get away clean because she believes that her reasons are justifiable. For your woman it's a reward for being under appreciated, disrespected, lacking affection, ignored, having the rules of the game switched behind her back.

Yes, we know that it is taught that men are the proud owners of the biggest egos, but I am here to teach you something different. Men are not the ones with the biggest egos; Women are.

On the subject of the female ego I have few and very simple things to say about this. Today's woman, not today's tramp, has been raised with strong parenting, and especially fathers or father figures, who have taught her to fall in love with herself first and foremost, and to believe that she is special in every way. With that upbringing comes a self-assured ego that demands to be nurtured.

It is a true statement that, "The man a girl holds in her life today, will be the man she holds in her future." Meaning that if she is daddy's little princess she will be attracted to a man that makes her feel like a queen when she becomes a woman. Although that statement is true, in most instances, remember that there are always exceptions in every situation.

You may be with a self respecting woman who was not raised by or around her dad or any other strong father figure but had a mom who did what dad should have done if he were around, you will get the same outcome if not a more self-assured woman.

Mommy's little princess can be even more egotistical because she was either raised by a woman who felt like she herself is a queen, a woman who will settle for nothing less when it comes to herself and especially when it comes to her beloved daughter. OR. She was raised by a woman who was not treated well and was belittled and suffered some sort of mistreatment by a man, therefore, she is going to do everything that she can in order to protect her daughters honor by making sure that her daughter does not suffer the same ill fate.

ZODIAC DICTATORS

Disclaimer: While all women are pretty much alike, I do honestly believe that zodiac signs dictate her level of secrecy.

Years ago one of the biggest pick up lines was, "What's your sign?" This was not just a conversation starter; it was actually a way to judge who you were meeting. I am firm believer that people do have not only natural genetic tendencies but they also have zodiac dictators. These dictators will tell you a lot about a woman. How much she will take, how kind, generous, serious, flirtatious, promiscuous, flighty, dedicated, mean, hard, and everything in between. Zodiac also dictates compatibility as it is sure that people do have zodiac dictators.

Think about the women you have dated in the past and what their zodiac signs were and if they had anything in common. Below I have given you a chart of zodiac and birthdays.

Aries the ram, March 21 – April 19
Taurus the bull, April 20 – May 20
Gemini the twins, May 21 – June 20
Cancer the crab, June 21 – July 22
Leo the lion, July 23 – August 22
Virgo the virgin, August 23 – September 21
Libra the scales, September 22 – October 23
Scorpio the scorpion, October 23 – November 21
Sagittarius the archer, November 22 – December 21
Capricorn the goat, December 22 – January 19
Aquarius the water bearer, January 20 – February 19
Pieces the fishes, February 20- March 20

Look at the chart and find your woman's birthday and zodiac. I'm not an astrologer so I will not break that down to you scientifically especially because there are hundreds of opinions out there about this subject matter. However, I will tell you that speaking from experience I do know that what is predicted 95% of the time is true about zodiac personality. I am a Scorpio and have read many things about the scorpion personality traits and I assure you that when I applied their prediction to myself, they are 95% if not 100% correct about my personality.

As I said, I am not going to go to crazy on this topic but I will give you a quick overview of personality traits for each. I would think that you should do more research on your own. The more information you have the better.

Aries – She is the first in the zodiac sign and is definitely woman who loves to venture out. She is a go-getter, often leading the way. She is usually confident, generous, fiery, bold, optimistic, and independent while being clingy or needy at the same time. She can also be moody, short tempered, self-involved, impulsive she sometimes leaves out the fine details which brings me to her being very impatient.

Taurus – She is not the one who really ventures out, she is a great leader follower and is there to make things better, in other words she is the one who dots the I's and crosses the t's. She has a great emotional strength, is practical, generous, and loyal but at the same time knows her limitations well. She on the other hand suffers from stubbornness, laziness, possessiveness, materialistic ways, and self-indulging.

Gemini - She is extremely independent and will not be pinned down by anyone or any rules as she needs to experience the world on her own. She is energetic, clever, imaginative, witty, and adaptable. But the problem with her is that she can be superficial, impulsive, restless, devious, and indecisive at times.

Cancer – She packed full with contradictions. She is very loyal, dependable, caring, adaptable, and responsive to needs of others. But she suffers from being moody, clingy, self-pitying, oversensitive, and self-absorbed at times. Side note on the cancer, a full moon is when her mood is best.

Leo – She is controlling and needs someone to admire her and appreciate her at all times. She is confident, sometimes over confident, ambitious, generous, loyal and encouraging. She also suffers from being pretentious, domineering, melodramatic, stubborn and vain which requires her to be the center of attention even when inappropriate.

Virgo – She is fully able to put her intelligence to use and get things done for herself. She is analytical, observant, helpful, reliable and precise. But she suffers from being skeptical, fussy, inflexible, interfering, and worst of all, cold.

Libra – She loves to be around other people. She is all about partnerships and groups. She is diplomatic, graceful, peaceful, idealistic, and hospitable. But she suffers from being superficial, vain, indecisive, and unreliable at times.

Scorpio – She is fiercely independent. She is able to accomplish anything she puts her mind to and she won't give up. She is not a social butterfly and is perfectly suited to be on her own. She is loyal, passionate, resourceful, observant, dynamic, and psychic. But suffers from being jealous, obsessive, suspicious, manipulative, and unyielding, therefore, she is not the one to cross and expect peace from.

Sagittarius – Independence is her principle this is why she craves adventure and excitement and welcome change with open arms. She is easily summed up as independent while suffering from being unemotional in return.

Capricorn – She is very independent because she knows her capabilities and therefore is rarely trusting of others to finish details for her. She is highly responsible, she is patient, ambitious, resourceful, and loyal to the mission at hand. But she suffers from being a dictator, being inhibited, conceited, distrusting, and unimaginative which can make her quite boring.

Aquarius – She is very independent. Any attempt to hold her down or restrict her will cause her to flee. She is witty, clever, a humanitarian, she is inventive, and original. She suffers from being stubborn, unemotional, sarcastic, rebellious, and aloof.

Pisces – She tends to need a dominant partner of role model in her life or she may very easily fall into a pit of self-pity and self-undoing. She will go out of her way for her loved ones as she is compassionate. She is adaptable, accepting, devoted, and imaginative. But she suffers from being oversensitive, indecisive, self-pitying, lazy, and an escapist so watch out!

When you read your woman's zodiac personality dictators, do you see anything familiar about her? Don't just focus on the negative, focus on the positive as well. I want you to realize once again that this is just a small and simple guide to what she is like.

When I look at this it definitely tells me who is and who is not a push over. I still suggest that you do more research so that you can get a better understanding of her and what makes her tick.

I also want you to realize that while thinking about her personality traits look at it from different angles. Take for instance the trait loyal. Don't think that only applies to you. It also applies to her and anything that she sets her mind to. Take clever, this means that she is using her brain and is undoubtedly a great planner. Take obsessive, this means that she is obsessed with getting what she feels is due, it doesn't mean obsessed with you. Take self-pitying, this does not mean she will wallow in her pain over you, this could be really dangerous because this makes her easily accessible le for some other man to come along and make her feel better quickly.

When you think about these traits, don't be narcissistic and apply them to helpful instances for yourself. Think of all the bad she can do with that good.

I say this to you my friend, in the words of a very good friend of mine, Mr. Harvey Levin, "Are you picking up what I'm putting down?"

MAKE HER STOP!

More than likely the woman who you have chosen to commit to is a woman who wants to be treated like a queen and by now you should know that there is only one way to happily be with a woman like that.

Treat her as such.

If you ever plan on being with any self respecting woman you need to get ready to treat her with kindness, love, and respect. Bouncing from one self-respecting woman to another will not fix your need to be unkind, loveless, and disrespectful to women. So unless you make the choice to be with a woman who has lower standards, you need to shape up and you need to do it now.

Be a *Man* about *Everything*

I am going to tell you some of the things that should be second nature when it comes to being a man. Unfortunately second nature doesn't always follow the first nature.

Just in case you are saying to yourself, 'How can you tell me how to be a man when you are a woman?' To answer that question, the reason I can tell you how to be a man is because I *am* a woman. In order to be a real man you have to be the polar opposite of a woman. Therefore, the first thing we have to do is kill your feminine ways, because believe me, any woman who wants to be with a man will never find you man enough for her.

Stop acting like her: I'm not talking about cross dressing or switching your hips or wearing makeup. I am talking about your other actions. Actions that you probably don't realize are very girly. Stop bitching and moaning about little things that are unimportant. If you have a disagreement, be a man about it. Settle the score and get over it. Don't walk around with a chip on your shoulder like a little woman who has no self-control.

Men are innately in control of all situations surrounding him. Men are not emotionally fragile. Men set the stage for what is to happen next. Men are rulers. Men are peace makers and peace keepers. On the other hand, women are the exact opposite. Women are innately in control of some, not all, situations surrounding her. Women are emotionally fragile. Women tend to perform on the stage that has been set by her man. This is why *men* run countries and women usually don't (Yes, I do realize Queen Elizabeth, but we all know she is surrounded my male leaders ruling with her voice) and with that I say, when it comes to the few women rulers around the world, if you take a glance, you will see that there is always a man hiding in the shadows and helping or directing her in how to make those massive, controlled, and unemotional choices needed to rule on a man's throne.

Stop being nitpicky and persnickety: By placing too much emphasis and being fussy about trivial and minor things, you look like a girly man versus a manly man. There is nothing more repulsive to a woman that a weak man that can't find anything masculine to do with his time other than nitpicking at her and everything around them. Now, I'm not talking about addressing things like having a clean house, nutritious foods prepared, and maybe even her poor health including her inclining weight (be gentle with that one guys) but I am talking about tiny things that I don't care to mention but will mention just in case there is a tiny mind reading this. A tiny thing is something like (the toothpaste cap, can good organization, junk drawer contents, the way she laughs, etc.) silly stuff. Stop it!

Show her that you are the Alpha Male: The best thing that you can do for yourself it to become an Alpha Male. Not only will your woman be completely attracted to you but so will the world that you live in.

For starters, it would be really simple for me to tell you to change but I am smart enough to know that change is not at all simple. In fact, I admit that I don't believe that people do or can actually change. I was once told by a teenage girl that 'people don't change, they just outgrow things' and I must say that she was right. Not only did she tell me that but she gave me an example. She explained that back when she was in second grade, if the teacher would put a math problem on the board and asked for the students to raise their hands in order to take a shot at solving the problem, she would jump in her seat and blurt out the answer. Although she does not have the same impulse to jump in her seat, being a college student now, she does however still say the answer out loud. She does not blurt the answer as she did when she was in the second grade, but her unsolicited response still escapes her lips. The moral to this story is that she has not changed. While she has outgrown jumping in her seat, she still has the personality to speak uncontrollably.

The other reasons I believe that (on average) people don't or won't change is because it is common knowledge that the average person simply hates change. There are many reasons that people hate change, and we could go on and on about it but for the sake of time and patience and the avoidance of sheer boredom, I am going to address the most common: Complacency, fear, and motivation.

I am addressing these three because they are exactly what we all suffer from in one form or another.

Complacency: We are comfortable and use to our routine. Even when the situation is not the most ideal, happy, or comfortable, we are still dumb enough to find comfort in the most idiotic, unhappy, or uncomfortable situations. By doing that we settle for whatever it is and don't make a move toward change.

Fear: The unknown equates to potential scary surprises. Believe it or not, there are many people who are daydreamers of success; be it in a professional or personal setting. We have all met people with lucrative ideas that never come to pass. We have also met many who have great relationship and life prescriptions but always seem to be unable to swallow their prescribed blue pill. The reason for their obvious failure is stemmed in their obvious fear of success. By not taking the prescribed blue pill, the person suffers symptoms of "self inflicted mistrust" which causes them to break out in insecurity, ultimately affecting all that they come in contact with.

Motivation: Having the stamina to make it to the finish line. Without proper stamina and endurance you will not be motivated enough to move forward into a better situation. I also realize that motivation will not be in place if you cannot find reasons compelling enough to propel you into a motivated mood. Because of this you will remain stifled and ready to just throw in the towel. This is not the way you should look at things in your life. The reason you should not look at things like this is because you will always stay in a losing position and never make it into a winning position.

I am certain that you were able to find at least one of these things within your personality. If you didn't, it's because you are being dishonest with yourself and your dishonesty is a blatant reflection of your fears and insecurities. Every human being is programmed with a flaw. No person is perfect and that includes you. Of course I and lots of other people would love to honestly say that we don't suffer any personality flaws but that would be an honest lie. If you can't find at least one of these flaws within yourself then kudos to you, you are a perfect person. But if you ask me and I'm sure your woman and children and acquaintances if you are flawed then welcome to the human race.

Today is your *new* birthday.

I know that you have met people, if not yourself, who would rather die before admitting wrongdoing or mistakes made. Those people are some of the saddest situations in the world because they will remain blind and never experience what could be wonderful.

But let's say that you did find some humanness within yourself and you are ready to make things better with your relationship, to you I say, let's get to work!

First address what the problem is. Do you cheat on her, are you insecure (about anything), are you simply comfortable, are you not motivated? Answer these questions.

Do you love her?

Are you in love her?

Do you like her?

If you answered a solid yes at least one of those three simple questions then you need to fix your relationship and stop her from cheating on you. I am almost certain that you answered no to at least one of the questions and my guess is that it was to the third question. If you answered no to the 'like her' question, that answer is understandable. Of course you wouldn't like her right now, and it's because she doesn't like you right now. Unless you have a mental problem and are chasing some woman who doesn't have any feelings for you, feelings between people are usually mutual. So by answering no to question number three, you know the reason why.

ALL IS FAIR IN LOVE AND WAR

This brilliant quote was spoken by John Lyly, a great Renaissance English poet in 1578. This is an unforgettable quote that has been used as justification for the foul things that take place during war and when in love.

Others have used similar quotes like "Turnabout is fair play" or "What's good for the goose is good for the gander." The later we have all heard over and over again when it comes to cheating. And if you think about it, it is a very true statement. Keeping things good for the female (goose) will keep things good for the male (gander). Be good to her and she will be good to you.

The unfortunate reality is that most men fail to understand those two quotes and what's even worse is that they fail to apply them to themselves. They would much rather use a quote like, "Two wrongs don't make a right." a quote that's nothing more than a failed attempt at licking clean the wounds of his bruised ego. For years men have quoted this one to women in hopes of getting her to stop acting like him, to stop cheating like him, and to stop disrespecting him like he disrespects her. Sorry fellas, this is another MANipulation that plays like a scratched CD.

I shared those quotes with you because I want you to consider the fact that she is not totally to blame. I want you to understand and man-up. Face facts and accept that you also had a big part in this relationship circling the drain.

If you fit into any of these categories mentioned in this book and you want to save your relationship, know that you can do just that. Please don't think that it is impossible to undo whatever damage that has been done.

Accept responsibility and take the punishment like a man. Don't dish out what you *don't* want to eat. If you put too much on her plate get ready to eat the leftovers whether you like your cooking or not.

I'm not going to tell you to completely change today, however, I am going to advise you to make big adjustments today. That's a big difference. Do what you should have never stopped doing. We all learned in college how to use critical thinking, and if you have not been to college or taken any critical thinking classes or philosophy classes. I suggest that you do.

We learned that change is a bad word in the minds of many people. Most humans have a difficult time dealing with change and usually will resist the notion of change at all cost if they could. So because the concept of change may be dreadful to you, and because it is urgent that something is done right away to fix your broken relationship, I'm going to tell you again to make adjustments!

Will she notice the difference?

Think about it. Have you ever known a person who you considered to be a lousy bum, a person who spoke the same words all the time, dressed the same, or walked around the same corners day in and day out? Now that you have brought this person to mind, I'm sure you consider this person to be someone you know very well.

Let's say that this person suddenly make's adjustments to their behavior. This person started speaking in complete sentences, wearing tailor made suits, started driving a brand new car down the main boulevard instead of walking around the same corners. If you were called to be a character witness on behalf of this person, your testimony would be a little confusing to you because you would not have one solid opinion of this person. You would have two separate opinions of him or her.

OR

You may still consider the person to be a bum dressed in great clothing riding in a new car. To you I would say that you are closed mined, and just as you would want your woman to have an open mind, you have to have one as well.

And, if you happen to be a guy that honestly did nothing wrong and she is cheating on you then there is another problem that must be addressed. It is likely to be that she simply doesn't want to be with you and have chosen to *not* tell you with words and is telling you with actions. To you I say cut your losses and move on as quickly as possible because STD's are no longer friendly little diseases that cooperate with antibiotics.

On the contrary...they kill!!

IT TAKES ONE TO KNOW ONE!

Unlike other "tackle-box"/"get-your-sh*t-together" books, I refuse to bore you with clinical studies and what statistics show. On the contrary, I am going to get straight to the point; that being the exact reason you picked up this book in the first place: To know why she does it and how she gets away with it.

I like to speak in a way that's easy to understand while using metaphors that are truly relatable. Because most men understand sports, in this book I am going to break this "cheating game" down like a game of basketball; first quarter second quarter and so forth and so on rules.

I am a real woman who happens to know lots of other real women and have had lots of real-women talk with those women; therefore, there is no better source than myself. I have also been wrapped up in holy matrimony that eventually turned unholy; and you know what they say: "You are your environment and adaptability is necessary". All that to say-while pleading the 5th on exact dates and times- I have firsthand knowledge of *"Why women do it and how they get away with it."*

ABOUT THE AUTHOR

Angelic Artiaga, a master wordsmith of vignettes, Angelic has lots of fun teasing her readers imaginations. Creating mysterious beginnings and orgasmic endings, her arousing imagery and vivid word-play always keeps her readers drooling for more.
Find out more at Amazon.com/author/AngelicArtiaga
Or visit AngelicArtiaga.com

OTHER BOOKS BY ANGELIC

Sinfullicious

Platinum Edition

Pure Erotica at its BEST!

www.ingramcontent.com/pod-product-compliance
Lightning Source LLC
Chambersburg PA
CBHW071735020426
42331CB00008B/2040